MOUSE

DUCK

WOODPECKER

FROG

DEER

BLACK BEAR

SKUNK

MUSKRAT

WOODCHUCK

OPOSSUM

PANTHER

BEAVER

THOMAS JEFFERSON'S BATTLE _for_ SCIENCE

BIAS, TRUTH, and a MIGHTY MOOSE!

A.   by BETH ANDERSON

B.   drawn by JEREMY HOLMES

Someone is coming!

CALKINS CREEK
AN IMPRINT OF ASTRA BOOKS FOR YOUNG READERS
New York

Bear

Weight = 410 pounds

PHILADELPHIA	
1776	
Jul. 4th	
6 am	68 °F
9 am	72 1/4 °F
1pm	76 °F
9pm	73 1/2 °F

1766	
	SHADWELL
Mar. 30.	Purple hyacinth —begins to bloom.

"There is not a sprig of grass that shoots uninteresting to me." — Thomas Jefferson

Mammoth

"The skeleton of the mammoth...bespeaks an animal of five or six times the cubic volume of the elephant."

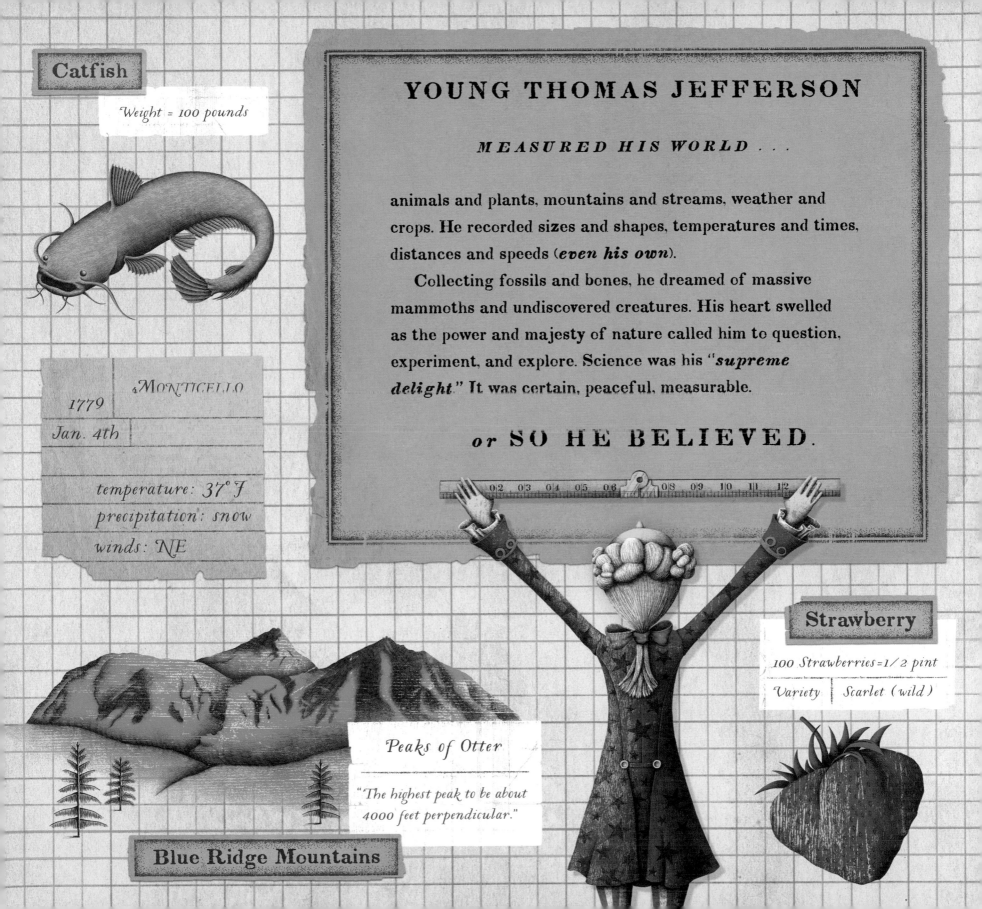

Catfish

Weight = 100 pounds

1779	*Monticello*
Jan. 4th	
temperature: 37° F	
precipitation: snow	
winds: NE	

YOUNG THOMAS JEFFERSON

MEASURED HIS WORLD . . .

animals and plants, mountains and streams, weather and crops. He recorded sizes and shapes, temperatures and times, distances and speeds (*even his own*).

Collecting fossils and bones, he dreamed of massive mammoths and undiscovered creatures. His heart swelled as the power and majesty of nature called him to question, experiment, and explore. Science was his "***supreme delight.***" It was certain, peaceful, measurable.

or SO HE BELIEVED.

02 03 04 05 06 07 08 09 10 11 12

Strawberry

100 Strawberries = 1/2 pint	
Variety	Scarlet (wild)

Peaks of Otter

"The highest peak to be about 4000 feet perpendicular."

Blue Ridge Mountains

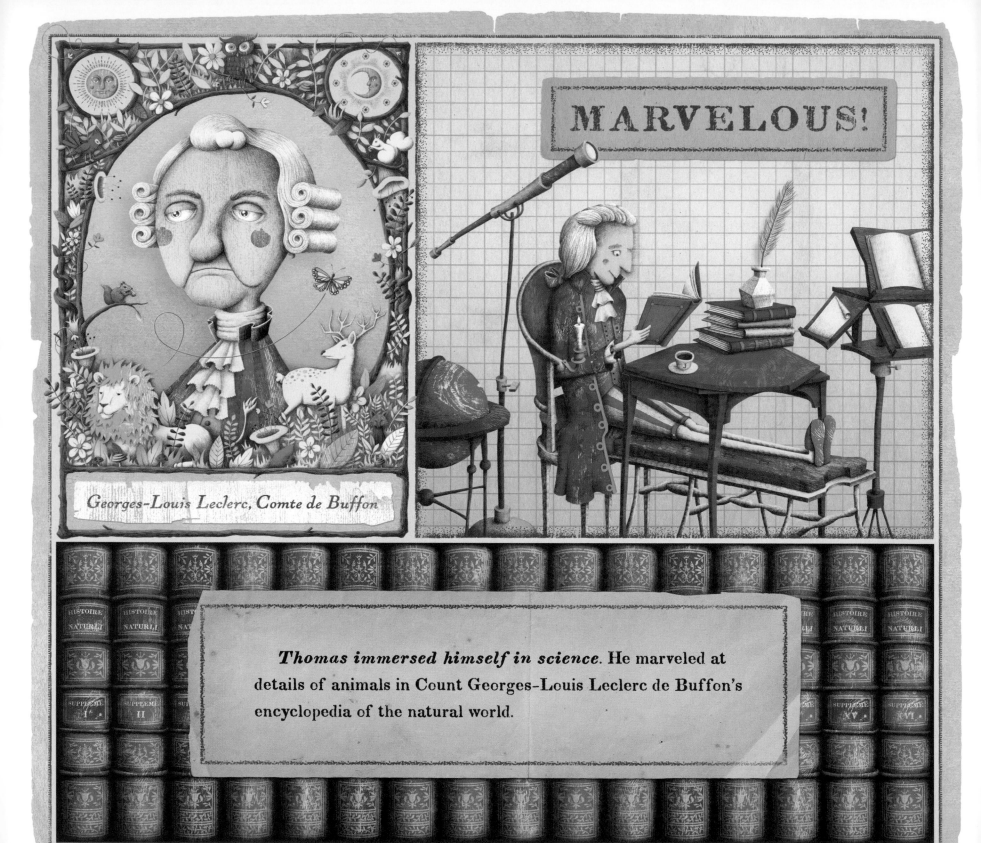

Georges-Louis Leclerc, Comte de Buffon

MARVELOUS!

Thomas immersed himself in science. He marveled at details of animals in Count Georges-Louis Leclerc de Buffon's encyclopedia of the natural world.

FURIOUS!

But when he read what the French scientist wrote about America, Thomas's fury flared, and the marvel melted away . . .

SUPPLEME
IX

BUFFON DECLARED

the NEW WORLD

was *swampy* and *cold*, with nothing as *grand*
as the elephant or *ferocious* as the lion.

HOGWASH!

America teemed with *grand* moose
and *ferocious* panthers.

BUFFON CLAIMED

bears were *smaller*, deer antlers *shorter*,
wolves downright *puny*.

ABSURD!

Since when did *bigger* mean *better*?

And when

BUFFON SAID

American mammoths were extinct, his words threatened Thomas's dream of one day finding the *"largest of all terrestrial beings."*

OuTrAgeOuS!

Thomas had samples of *teeth*! And *bones*! How could such a behemoth *disappear*?

PAGE *after* PAGE,

the ROYAL SCIENTIST PROCLAIMED

America a terrible place. Far worse than the Old World of Europe and Asia.

WOoF!

PoPpYCoCK!

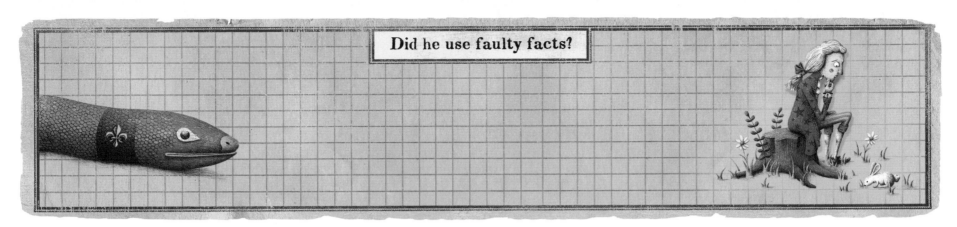

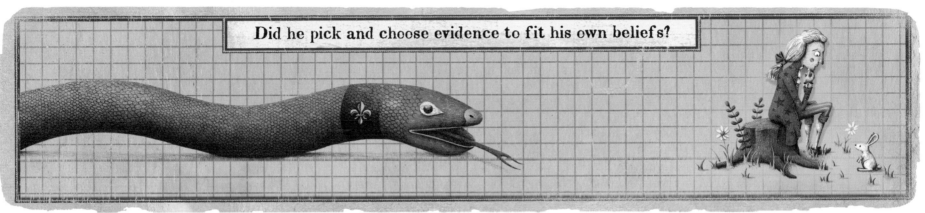

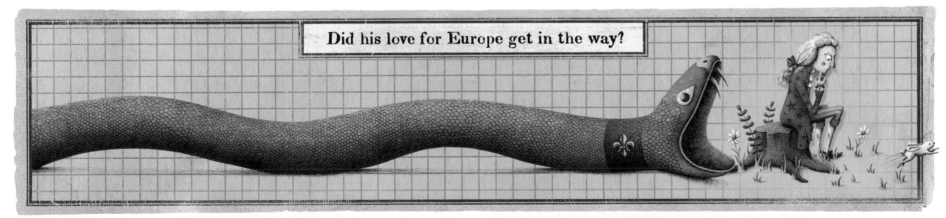

SUDDENLY SCIENCE
WASN'T CERTAIN.
OR PEACEFUL.

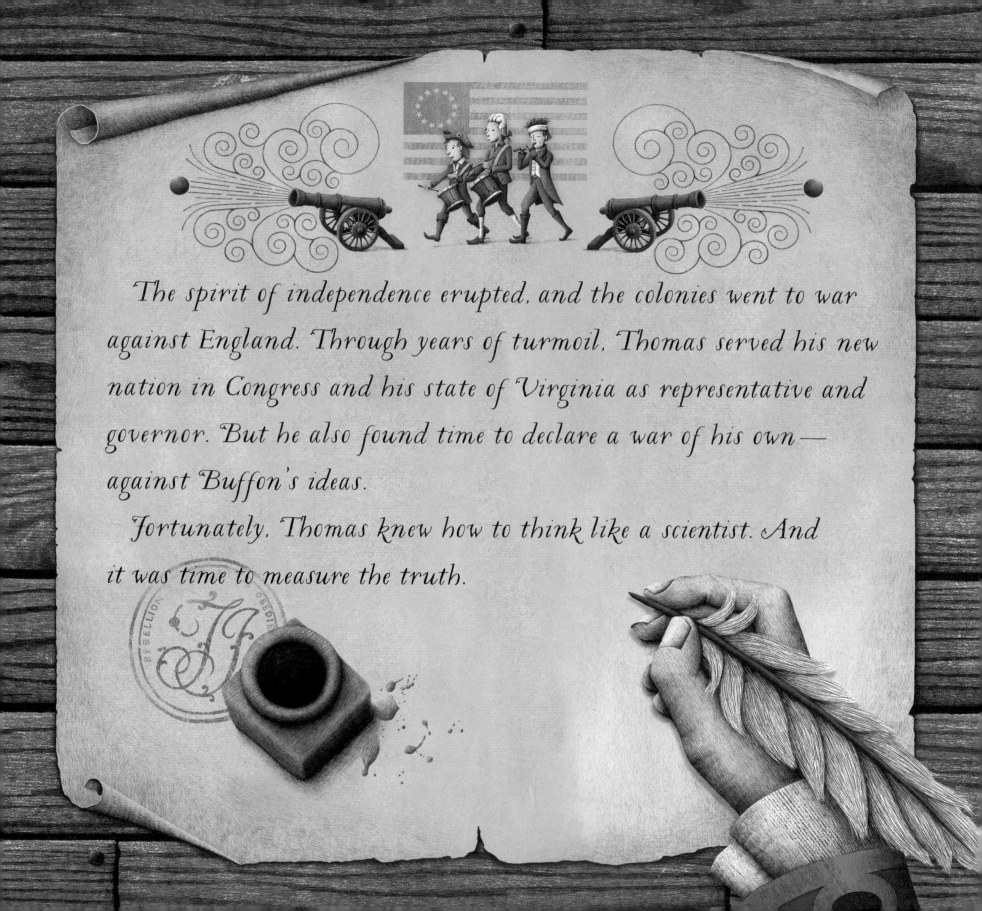

The spirit of independence erupted, and the colonies went to war against England. Through years of turmoil, Thomas served his new nation in Congress and his state of Virginia as representative and governor. But he also found time to declare a war of his own—against Buffon's ideas.

Fortunately, Thomas knew how to think like a scientist. And it was time to measure the truth.

TIME to FIGHT
for LIBERTY!

TIME to FIGHT
for the TRUTH!

QUESTION 01 — Was Buffon confusing deer and moose, cougars and panthers?

QUESTION 02 — How did he determine that mammoths were extinct?

WHERE DID THE SCIENTIST

get his information if he had never been to

AMERICA?

THOMAS looked closer. Buffon had relied on the notes of travelers. "*Did they measure or weigh the animals . . .?*" Thomas asked. Or "*mistake the species*"?

1748 Philadelphia

"Bears are very numerous higher up in the country, and do much mischief Mr. Bartram told me that when a bear catches a cow, he kills her in the following manner he bites into the a hole hide, and blows with all his power into it, and dies. till the animal swells excessively

— Peter Kalm

If he could prove the numbers were wrong, Buffon's whole theory would fall apart! Thomas devised a plan.

He created a list of four-legged animals from Europe and America. Focusing on **BIG**, he organized the quadrupeds from largest to smallest. Then he sent a dispatch to friends from north to south: send "*the heaviest weights of our animals . . . from the mouse to the mammoth.*"

Dear John, Ben George, James...

One war down, one to go!

As the war for independence ended, Thomas's war on faulty facts continued. He verified data, analyzed numbers, and drew conclusions.

Even without the weight of a mammoth, he had enough evidence to prove Buffon wrong.

NOTES ON THE STATE OF VIRGINIA.

And prove it, he would—with his **own** book! Thomas's thoughts boomed as his pen marched across the pages:

A	describing wildlife in America.
B	attacking falsehoods.
C	quashing Buffon's theory.

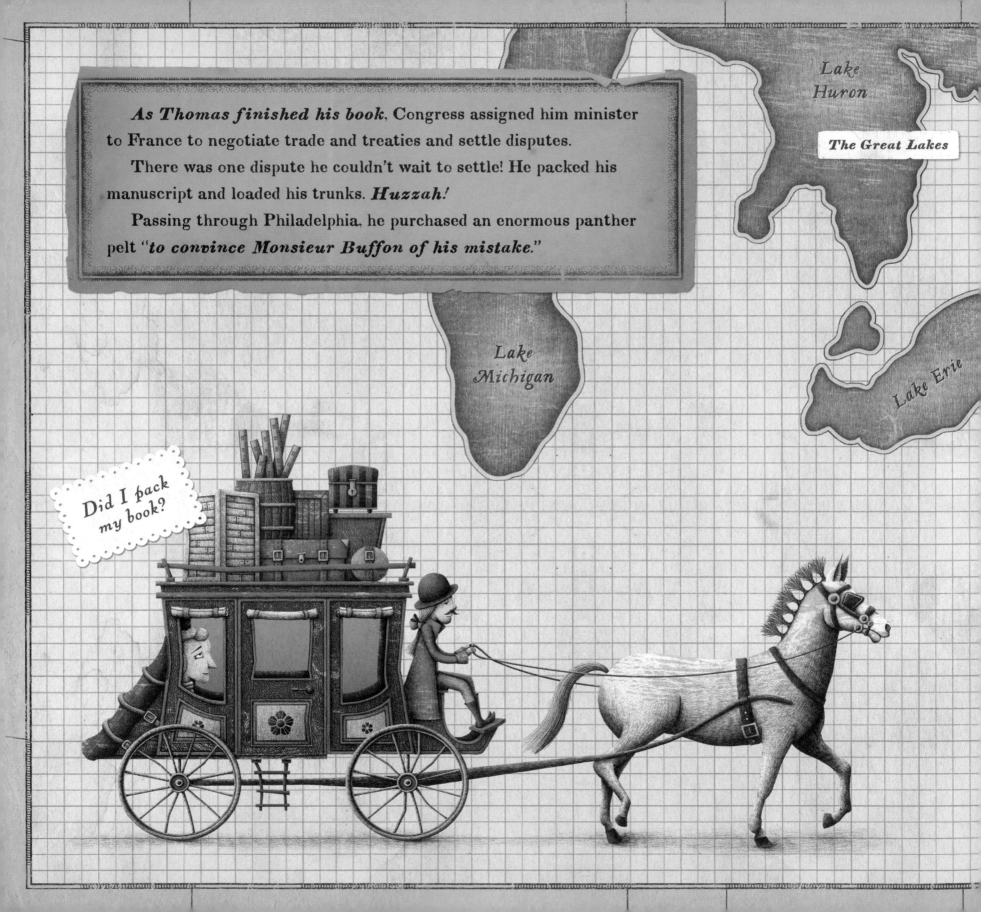

As Thomas finished his book, Congress assigned him minister to France to negotiate trade and treaties and settle disputes.

There was one dispute he couldn't wait to settle! He packed his manuscript and loaded his trunks. *Huzzah!*

Passing through Philadelphia, he purchased an enormous panther pelt "*to convince Monsieur Buffon of his mistake.*"

The Great Lakes

Lake Huron

Lake Michigan

Lake Erie

Did I pack my book?

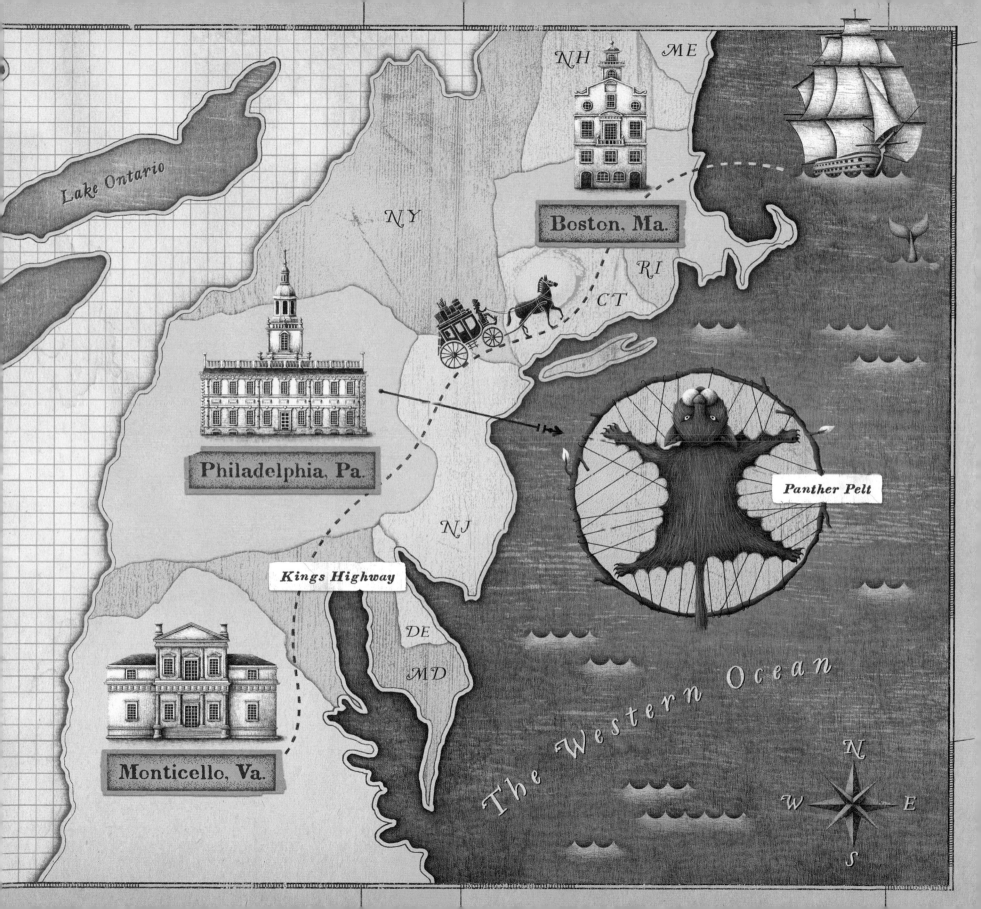

Lake Ontario

NH

ME

NY

Boston, Ma.

RI

CT

Philadelphia, Pa.

Panther Pelt

NJ

Kings Highway

DE

MD

The Western Ocean

Monticello, Va.

N
W   E
S

While Thomas tended to business in Paris, he waited to meet Buffon . . .

One month.

Five months.

Ten months passed.

Thomas had his book printed and sent off a copy to Buffon.

More

months

passed.

Thomas sent the panther skin.

to Thomas Jefferson
Hôtel de Langeac
92, avenue
des Champs-Élysées

Cougar skin?

WHAT WOULD IT TAKE
to convince Buffon of his errors?

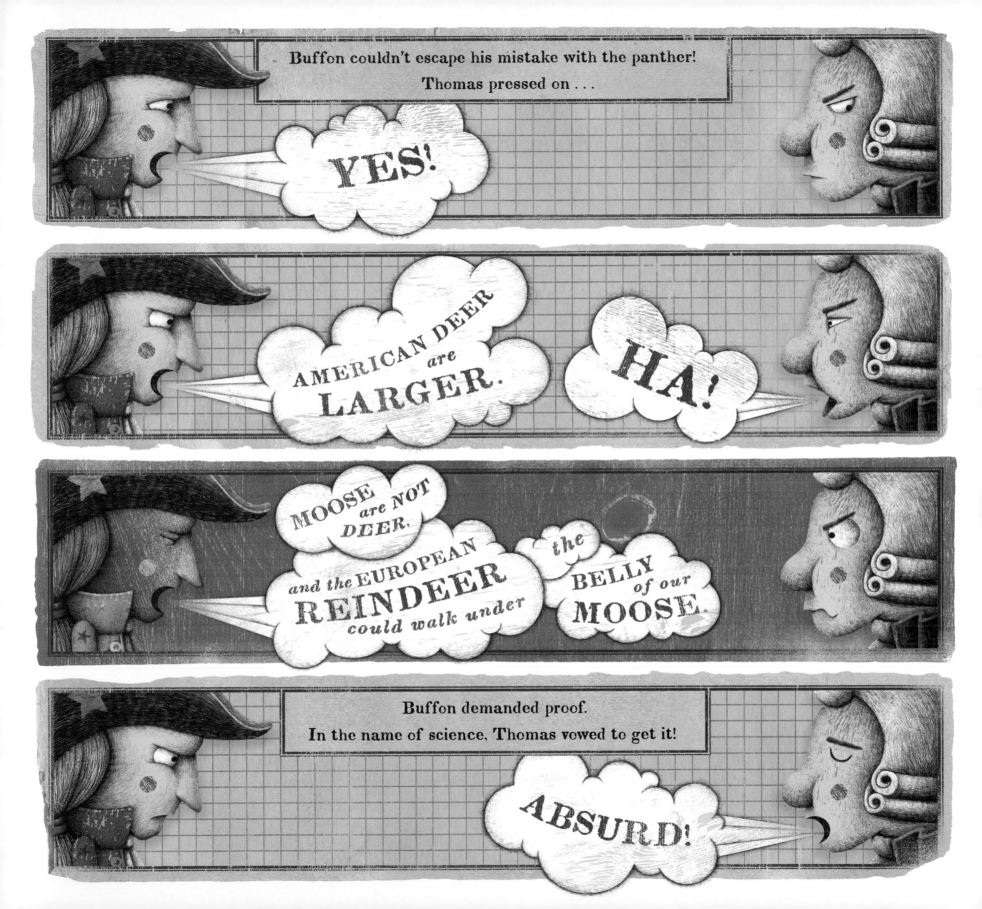

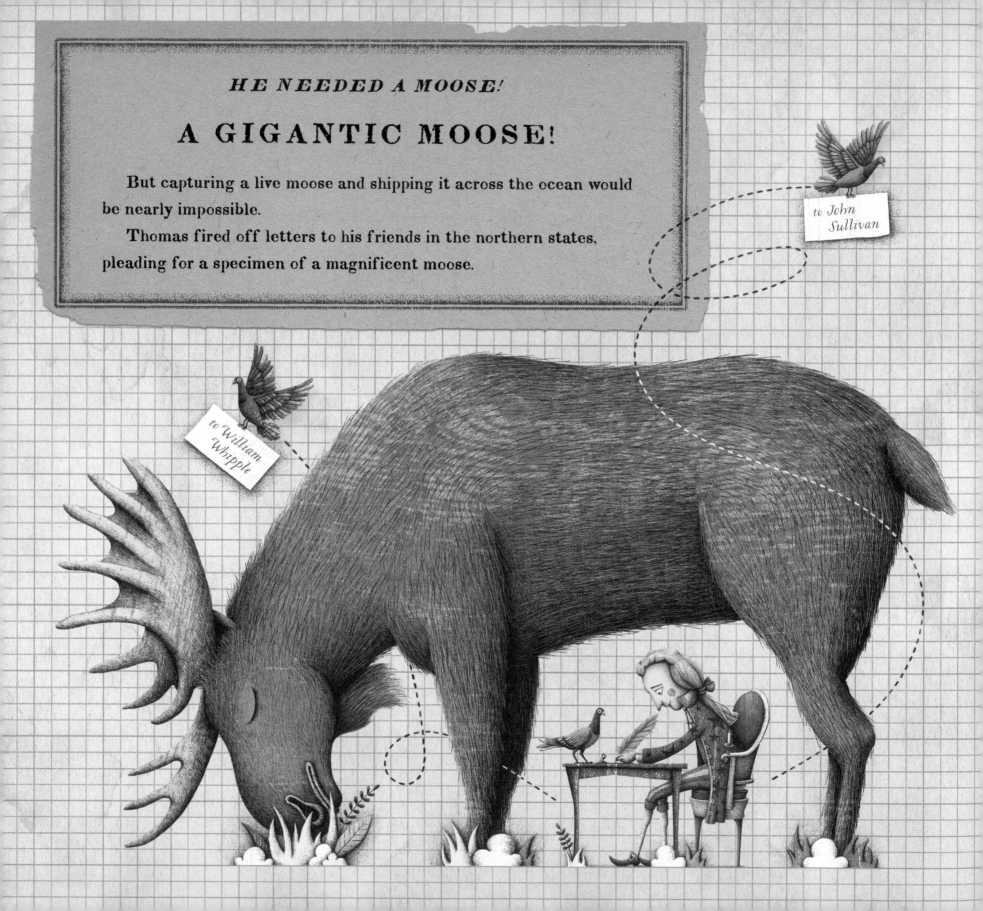

HE NEEDED A MOOSE!

A GIGANTIC MOOSE!

But capturing a live moose and shipping it across the ocean would be nearly impossible.

Thomas fired off letters to his friends in the northern states, pleading for a specimen of a magnificent moose.

to John Sullivan

to William Whipple

NOTES
ON THE
STATE of VIRGINIA

BY THOMAS JEFFERSO[N]

His Excellency Thos. Jefferson Esqr. To Jno.

	2[8]	13	2
1787 To paid Capt. Robert Colburn for the Skeleton of a moose and Transporting to Durham	3	15	0
To a pair of moose horns and Expence of procuring them	2	10	0
To a pair of Elks horns & expence of procuring	1	10	0
To a pair of Deers horns & expence of procuring	3	15	0
To a pair of Carribous Horns & Expence of procuring	2	14	0
To expence of cleansing the Skeleton from flesh and salting and tending the same to prevent putrefaction	-	12	0
To paid a Tanner for fleshing the Skins	2	18	0
To paid Expence of Dressing the Skins to preserve it with the hair on, free from worms &c with expence of Allum brick, Dust & Tobacco	-	16	0
To paid Expence of a Box and putting up the skeleton &c	-	12	0
To expence of sending the Box to Portsmouth	-	18	0
...d for horns of the Spike hornd Buck		0	0
...13 times sending to Effingham ...the province of Main, to		4	0
...t Durham and		17	
		46	7

UMPH!

Let's hope the moose is as BIG as the bill.

After a year and a half, he had all but given up when a gigantic bill arrived for the pursuit, preparation, and transport of a moose.

BUT WHERE WAS THE MOOSE?

Soon more letters came. Thomas cringed as he read of the "***very troublesome affair***":

A.	*involving twenty men*
B.	*hauling a seven-foot-tall animal*
C.	*for fourteen days*
D.	*through deep snow*
E.	*and twenty miles of forest.*

A FEW DAYS LATER, a colossal box arrived—with a monstrous stench.

Thomas peered at the moose. Not magnificent, but BIG. He sent it off, with apologies for the moose's hair and mismatched antlers.

Buffon's response came with a promise **TO REVISE HIS BOOK!**

But when Thomas received news of the royal scientist's death a few months later, he feared Buffon's faulty facts would never be corrected.

THOMAS RETURNED HOME and continued his fight for science.

But this time, he wasn't alone. His book had found its way into the hands of young and old.

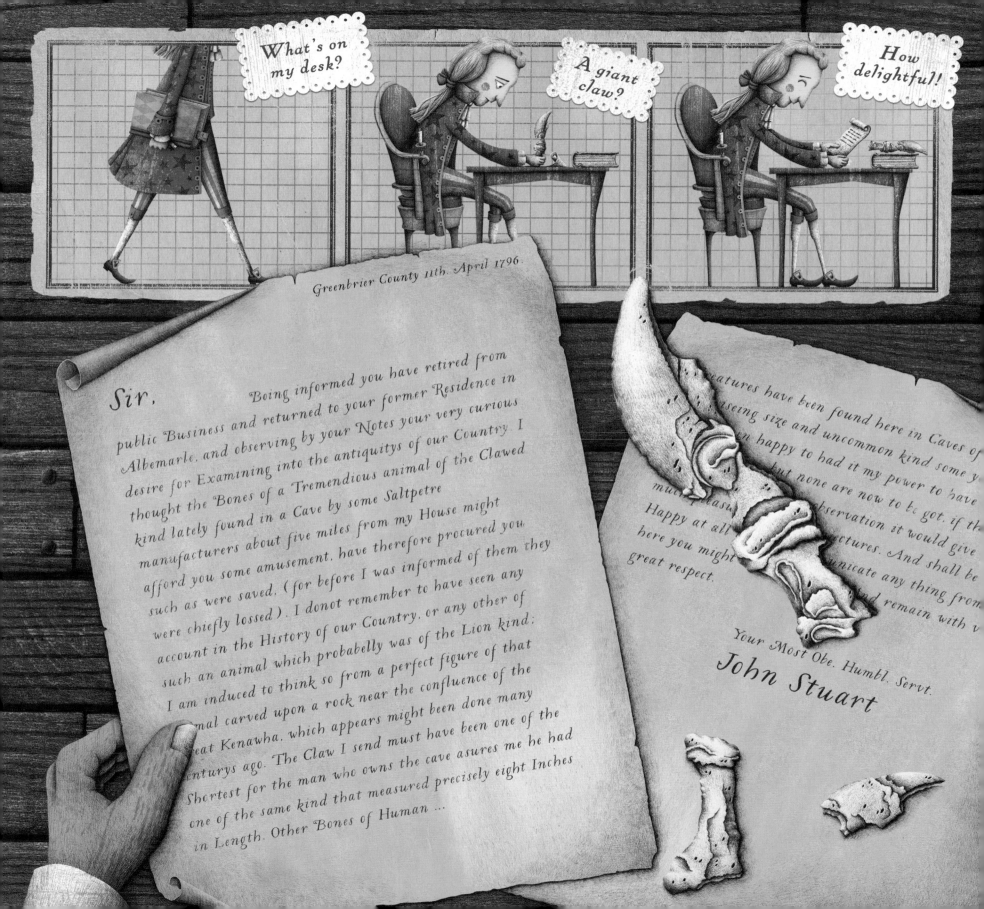

Peaks of Otter

he highest peak

00 feet perp

NOTES

ON THE

STATE OF VIRGINIA

WITH AN

APPENDIX.

BY THOMAS JEFFERSON.

A.	Measuring and collecting.
B.	Experimenting and exploring.
C.	Questioning and verifying.

THOMAS JEFFERSON LED THE WAY.

Year after year, facts and discoveries piled up. But no mammoths. The massive beast was indeed extinct. But that single drop of disappointment didn't dampen Thomas's unspeakable joy in science.

"There is not a sprig of grass that shoots
uninteresting to me." — Thomas Jefferson

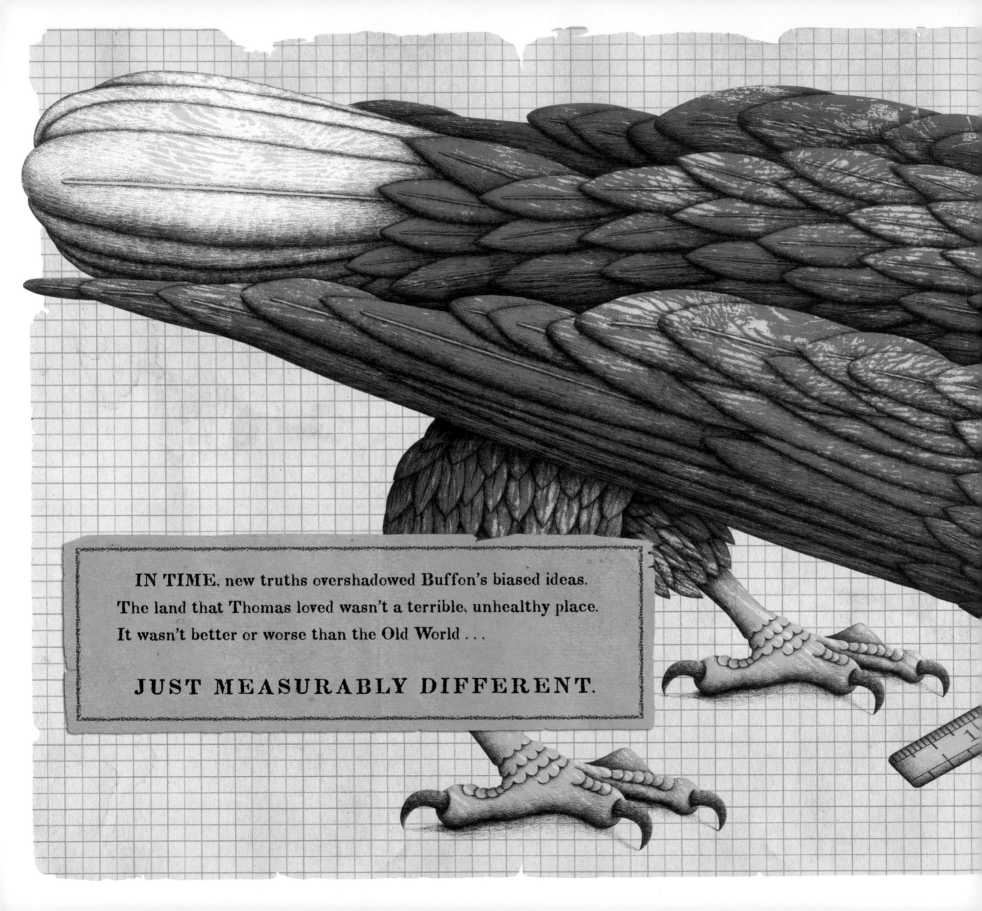

IN TIME, new truths overshadowed Buffon's biased ideas. The land that Thomas loved wasn't a terrible, unhealthy place. It wasn't better or worse than the Old World . . .

JUST MEASURABLY DIFFERENT.

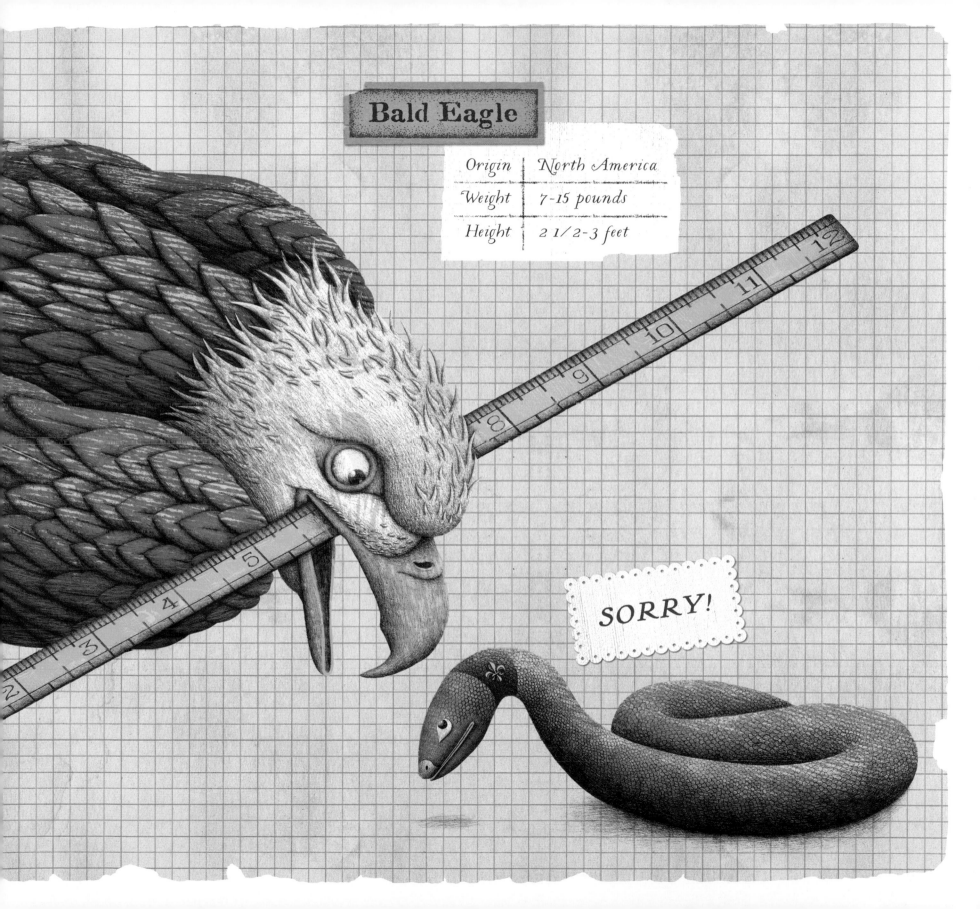

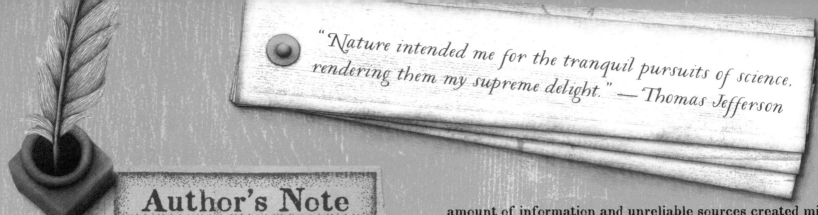

Author's Note

While Thomas Jefferson, one of the most famous Founding Fathers, dutifully served his country in many positions, his mind was always on science. Notepad in his pocket, he constantly measured, examined, experimented, and explored. Even on July 4, 1776, one of the most important days in the country's history, he recorded the temperature four times.

Jefferson was interested in all branches of science, especially natural history. As president, he displayed his large collection of bones and fossils in the East Room of the White House, creating his own small museum. When he left the presidency and retired to Monticello, he filled the entrance hall with artifacts, inventions, and art. Later, intent on sharing the joys of science and the pursuit of knowledge, Thomas Jefferson established the University of Virginia.

Count Buffon was trying to figure out how and why animals were the way they were. In the 1700s, no one knew very much about the world, and there was much to be learned. What appears in this story is one small part of Buffon's theory that said the New World of America was an unhealthy environment. It seems clear that he loved Europe so much that he used science to support his belief that it was a superior land. This is called confirmation bias. Instead of searching for truth, he was trying to prove what he already believed.

Jefferson and other Americans felt Buffon's theory about the New World threatened the future of the soon-to-be United States at a time when they hoped for immigrants and trade. As an amateur scientist, Jefferson understood how a limited amount of information and unreliable sources created mistruths. He understood how easily people were fooled when these ideas came from someone with power and authority. He also understood how hard it was to get rid of misinformation once it spread. Buffon's ideas took more than a century to completely fade away.

Mistruths are created in many ways, such as outright lies, lack of information, faulty reasoning, and biases based on opinions, traditions, pride, power, and greed. Some mistruths might be seen as harmless, but many are dangerous. Far worse than Buffon's ideas about animals were ideas that tried to use science to claim that some races of people were inferior and could be treated as less than human. We cannot ignore the fact that Jefferson, the author of the Declaration of Independence, which states the larger human truth that "all men are created equal," was a slave owner. Looking at Jefferson as a scientist, it's hard to understand why he didn't fight back against the senseless reasoning. His thinking, too, was biased.

In 1803, after the country acquired a huge piece of land from the French in the Louisiana Purchase, Jefferson launched an expedition to explore the new territory to the west. He insisted that the men be trained in gathering information to avoid the mistakes that Buffon had made and was overjoyed when they returned with a treasure trove of discoveries. But the scientific quest had larger effects Jefferson didn't consider. When it opened up the West to settlement, the Native peoples living there, including the Osage, Sioux, Cheyenne, Crow, Mandan, Blackfeet, Shoshone, and Nez Perce tribes, lost their lives, lands, and culture.

Just as Buffon wasn't right about everything, Thomas Jefferson wasn't either. What he thought was a lion, and named "giant claw" or *Megalonyx*, turned out to be the giant sloth. What he insisted were distinct species, the panther and cougar, we now recognize as one. What he called the mammoth was later determined to be a mastodon. Jefferson and many others believed extinction was impossible, that there was an unbreakable Chain of Being—until Lewis and Clark returned and reported no living mammoths. With this new information, Jefferson admitted Buffon was right and accepted that extinction was real.

Scientific truth is always changing and growing as we discover more about our world. Science isn't always peaceful or certain, easy or convenient, what we wanted or what we believed. As we advance genetic engineering, address climate change, and experiment with artificial intelligence, will we consider the far-reaching consequences of our actions? Will we face the challenges of justice and larger human truths—truths that can only be measured with the heart? With diverse voices bringing together wide experiences, we have a better chance of a bright future.

Thomas Jefferson had giant-moose-size hopes that future generations would carry science forward and fight back against faulty facts and biases with scientific thinking.

"When I contemplate the immense advances in science, and discoveries in the arts which have been made within the period of my life, I look forward with confidence to equal advances by the present generation; and have no doubt they will consequently be as much wiser than we have been, as we than our fathers were." —Thomas Jefferson

SCIENTIFIC INQUIRY
PROCESS

THOMAS JEFFERSON'S PROCESS OF *"MEASURING TRUTH"* WAS MUCH LIKE WHAT STUDENTS ARE TAUGHT TODAY.

STEP 1 Ask questions. Identify one that can be answered through scientific investigation.

STEP 2 Plan and conduct a scientific investigation.

STEP 3 Use tools, equipment, and observation to gather, analyze, and interpret data.

STEP 4 Draw conclusions based on data.

STEP 5 Communicate your findings.

Timeline *of* Thomas Jefferson's Life

1743	Thomas Jefferson born in Shadwell, Virginia.
1760–62	Attends College of William & Mary.
1769–74	Serves in the Virginia House of Burgesses (Virginia legislature).
1772	Marries Martha Wayles Skelton.
1775	Elected to second Continental Congress. Revolutionary War begins.
1776	Drafts the Declaration of Independence.
1776–79	Serves in the Virginia House of Delegates.
1779–81	Serves as governor of Virginia. Receives a questionnaire from the French asking for information on Virginia, which is later expanded into his book, *Notes on the State of Virginia*.
1781	British attack Virginia and Monticello, his home. Jefferson and his family escape. In December, he begins writing the book, *Notes on the State of Virginia*.
1782	His wife, Martha, dies.
1783	Elected to Congress again. War ends in September.
1784	Finishes his book. Sent to France as a foreign minister.
1785	In May, gets two hundred copies of his book printed. Sends a copy to Buffon in June. Sends the panther skin in December. December 31, receives Buffon's invitation to dinner.
1786	Early January, dines with Buffon. January 7, writes for a moose specimen.
1787	*Notes on the State of Virginia* published in US. October 1, Jefferson sends moose to Buffon.
1789	September, Jefferson returns to the US.
1790–93	Secretary of State under George Washington.
1797–1801	Vice President under John Adams.
1801–09	President of the US.
1803	Louisiana Purchase.
1803–06	Lewis and Clark and the Corps of Discovery Expedition.
1809	Retires from public office and goes home to Virginia.
1817	Lays the cornerstone for future University of Virginia.
1826	Dies at Monticello on July 4.

Bibliography

All quotations used in the book can be found in the following sources marked with an asterisk (*).

PRIMARY SOURCES

Buffon, Georges-Louis Leclerc, Comte de. *The Natural History of Quadrupeds*, Vol. 2–3. Edinburgh: Thomas Nelson and Peter Brown, 1830. HathiTrust Digital Library.

*Jefferson, Thomas. *Notes on the State of Virginia*. John Stockdale, opposite Burlington-House, Piccadilly, 1787. Google Books, original from Oxford University, digitized March 31, 2009.

*———. "The Papers of Thomas Jefferson." National Archives. founders.archives.gov/about/Jefferson [multiple letters].

*Webster, Daniel, and Edwin David Sanborn. *The Private Correspondence of Daniel Webster*, Vol. 1. Boston: Little, Brown, 1856.

Wiltse, Charles M., and Harold D. Moser, eds. "The Papers, 1798–1824." In *The Papers of Daniel Webster: Correspondence: Volume 1: 1798–1824*. Hanover, NH: University Press of New England, 1974, 370–82.

SECONDARY SOURCES

Bedini, Silvio A. *Jefferson and Science*. Chapel Hill: University of North Carolina Press, 2002.

———. *Thomas Jefferson: Statesman of Science*. New York: Macmillan, 1990.

"Buffon's American Degeneracy: Part 1: Old World vs. New." The Academy of Natural Sciences. Philadelphia: Drexel.

Coburn, Mark. "A Moose for the Misinformed: Jefferson and Natural History." *American Heritage* 62, no. 3 (Summer 2017).

Dugatkin, Lee Alan. *Mr. Jefferson and the Giant Moose: Natural History in Early America*. Chicago: University of Chicago Press, 2009.

———. "Thomas Jefferson Defends America With a Moose." *Slate Magazine*, September 12, 2012.

*———. "Thomas Jefferson Versus Count Buffon: The Theory of New World Degeneracy." *Chautauqua Journal* 1, article 17 (2016).

Kimball, Marie. *Jefferson War and Peace 1776–1784*. New York: Coward-McCann, 1947.

Klinghard, Daniel, and Dustin Gish. *Thomas Jefferson and the Science of Republican Government: A Political Biography of "Notes on the State of Virginia."* Cambridge: Cambridge University Press, 2017.

Krulwich, Robert. "Thomas Jefferson Needs A Dead Moose Right Now To Defend America." NPR, January 16, 2014.

Martin, Edwin Thomas. *Thomas Jefferson: Scientist*. New York: Collier Books, 1961.

Martin, Travis. "Thomas Jefferson, Scientist." *Journal of the American Revolution*, August 20, 2015.

Mooallem, Jon. *Wild Ones: A Sometimes Dismaying, Weirdly Reassuring Story about Looking at People Looking at Animals in America*. New York: Penguin Books, 2013.

Semonin, Paul. *American Monster: How the Nation's First Prehistoric Creature Became a Symbol of National Identity*. New York: New York University Press, 2000.

Thomson, Keith. "Jefferson, Buffon, and the Moose." *American Scientist* 96, no. 3 (2008): 200–02.

———. *Jefferson's Shadow: The Story of His Science*. New Haven, CT: Yale University Press, 2012.

Wilson, Gaye. "Jefferson, Buffon, and the Mighty American Moose." *Monticello Newsletter* 13 (Spring 2002).

Wulf, Andrea. "Thomas Jefferson's Quest to Prove America's Natural Superiority." *Atlantic*, March 7, 2016.

Zechmeister, Gene, and John Ragosta. "Notes on the State of Virginia." Thomas Jefferson Encyclopedia, Monticello.org. Revised February 22, 2018.

Acknowledgments

Thank you to the many scholars who have researched and written about Thomas Jefferson and also to archivists and historians who have preserved, catalogued, and digitized his many letters. Immense gratitude to Gaye Wilson, Senior Historian, Robert H. Smith International Center for Jefferson Studies at Monticello, for reviewing the manuscript. Heartfelt thanks to my agent, Stephanie Fretwell-Hill; editor, Carolyn Yoder; and stalwart critique partners Julie, Kristen, Ann, Kristen, Brooke, Michelle, Heather, Vivian, Hannah, and Kristin. And as always, love and appreciation to my family for their enthusiastic support through this writing journey.

For Dave, with gratitude — *BA*
For Jennifer, Paxton, Charlie, Paris,
and Tim — *JH*

Calkins Creek
An imprint of Astra Books for Young Readers, a division of Astra Publishing House
astrapublishinghouse.com

Printed in China

ISBN: 978-1-63592-620-0 (hc)
ISBN: 978-1-63592-862-4 (eBook)
Library of Congress Control Number: 2022949702

First edition
10 9 8 7 6 5 4 3 2 1

Design by Barbara Grzeslo
The text is set in Webster Roman WF.
The titles are set in Webster Roman WF.
The illustrations are woodblock prints and digital pencil.

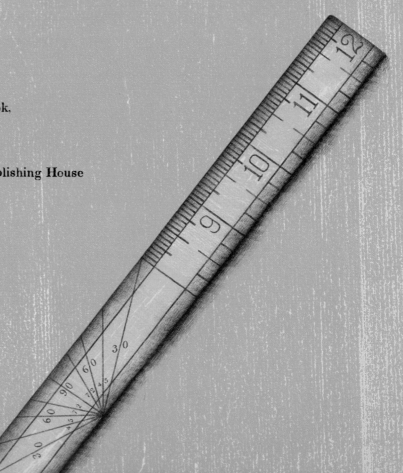

MOUSE

DUCK

WOODPECKER

FROG

BLACK BEAR

DEER

SKUNK

MUSKRAT

WOODCHUCK

OPOSSUM

PANTHER

BEAVER